My Friend & My King

MY FRIEND & MY KING

John's Vision of Our Hope of Heaven

CALVIN MILLER

Illustrated by Ron Mazellan

Chariot Victor Publishing
A Division of Cook Communications

Chariot Victor Publishing,
a division of Cook Communications,
Colorado Springs, Colorado 80918
Cook Communications, Paris, Ontario
Kingsway Communications, Eastbourne, England

MY FRIEND & MY KING
© 1999 by Calvin Miller for text and Ron Mazellan for illustrations.

Cover and interior design by Peter Schmidt of Granite Design
Illustrations by Ron Mazellan
Editor: Karen Artl

First printing, 1999
Printed in Singapore
03 02 01 00 99   5 4 3 2 1

Library of Congress Cataloging-in-Publication Data
Miller, Calvin.
        My friend & my king : John's vision of our hope of heaven
/ Calvin Miller ; illustrated by Ron Mazellan.
        p.   cm.
        Summary: A simplified version of the story of John's
vision of the future of the world and God's ultimate triumph as
revealed to him by Jesus.
        ISBN 0-7814-3315-0
        1. Bible stories, English—N.T. Revelation. [1. Bible.
N.T. Revelation Paraphrases.] I. Mazellan, Ron, ill. II. Title.
III. Title: My friend and my King.
BS2825.5.M55   1999
228' .09505—dc21   99-28723
                                                 CIP

Published in association with the literary agency of Alive
Communications, Inc., 1465 Kelly Johnson Blvd., Suite 320,
Colorado Springs, CO 80920

To Andrew & Jared
C.M.

For Jil and my boys, Nathan, Kyle, and Evan.
I am truly blessed.

R.M.

———————— ❧ ————————

This book represents one author's attempt to make
the Book of Revelation and Jesus' Second Coming
understandable to children. The Book of Revelation
remains somewhat a mystery, and it is best to read a book
like this in conjunction with actual Bible text.

"Here I am! I stand at the door and knock.

If anyone hears my voice and opens the door,

I will come in and eat with him, and he with me.

To him who overcomes, I will give the right to

sit with me on my throne, just as I overcame

and sat down with my Father on his throne."

Revelation 3:20-21 (NIV).

My name is John. It was my joy and privilege to be a disciple of our Lord and Savior, Jesus. I wish I could describe for you how much that means to me! He was my teacher, my guide, and my friend. I'd like to share an experience I had with Jesus some years after His death, when I was in prison on the island of Patmos.

I was alone one Sunday, thinking about how much I would like to be with my friend Jesus again. Many years had passed since His death and resurrection, and I longed to see Him once more. Suddenly, I heard the blast of a trumpet behind me! The sheer loudness startled me and caused me to spin around.

There He stood! Jesus! Jesus, my friend! I had waited for Him for so long. I gazed upon Him. My eyes brimmed with tears of joy. *It is you*, my trembling brain cried to my thumping, terrified heart.

He was no longer that simple man-like Christ I had known so many years ago. He had gloriously changed. Now He seemed taller, grander, more king-like. His eyes were like fire. His clothes were shining like they were made of shimmering moonlight and glistening sunlight interwoven on the same great celestial loom. He spoke and His words rang clear and majestic. He was a study in splendor, a picture of power.

I wanted to shout, "You have come for me. Is this your glorious Second Coming?"

"No," He said simply. "I have come to tell future events to you."

I fell to the earth with my face to the ground.

Jesus reached down, placed His hand on my shoulder, lifted me upward and turned my face toward His.

"I've come to tell you about all the things that are going to happen. What you see and hear, write in a book."

Then He showed me the door that leads into heaven. "Come with Me," He said, and it seemed we flew as freely as birds do. Up, up, up, we soared high above the island. We seemed to circle through the universe to the galactic edges of the stars. Then, we actually went through a great door that led us into the court of God.

I had long wondered what heaven would be like. Now I was seeing it first hand. It is nearly impossible to describe this wonderful place, the glistening grace, the crystal, towering splendor of it all. There were thousands upon thousands of singing creatures, and Jesus Himself was the focus of the music. All the court of heaven raised anthems of praise to Jesus, my friend, the King.

His love had brought me to this wonderful place. His love had done it all! Yet, His love did not do its best work in this place. Here in this splendid light His love was obvious, but it had proved its worth on the planet where He was once crucified and I was still imprisoned.

Suddenly, all of time flashed before me. Jesus began to show me vision after vision of those terrible events that would befall the earth. I saw endless rulers who led their cruel hordes of soldiers on deadly marches across the earth conquering nations in their military campaigns. Nations rose and fell, and still the lust for power made rulers wage war after war upon the innocent.

I began to weep quietly in my despair. I tried to write of these sufferings as He had instructed me, but my tears slowed the writing of the sometimes glorious, sometimes awful, revelation.

This frightful battle, this bloody Armageddon was too awful for words. *How long will evil rulers control the world,* I wondered to myself. *O Christ, my King and friend,* I prayed in my heart, *let it not be so!*

Then I heard a multitude of angels cry:

Hallelujah! Salvation and glory and power and honor belong to our God.

I raised my head and I cried out to them in a soundless voice, "Will the dark lord, Satan, always terrorize the earth?"

A single, bold cry of a powerful angel responded with a triumphant, "Never!" Then a chorus of angels sang out again, "Hallelujah, for the Lord God Almighty reigns. Let us rejoice and be glad and give Him the glory!"

My deep despair brightened with new hope.

I smiled, I laughed. "Hallelujah," I shouted, echoing the angels, "the Lord God Almighty reigns!" I took up my pen again and began to write with words that flew from my mind to my pen to the scroll.

*R*ejoicing in Christ's victory on one hand, I couldn't help but wonder then what would happen to the dark lord, Satan. No sooner did I have that thought than I received the vision of Satan as he was thrown into a lake of destruction. Even as he perished, a huge, steely wall closed over his leering, ugly form. He was gone! He would never return!

The war to end all wars was finally over. Evil was forever purged from the earth!

Then I saw Jesus as the great, kind, conquering King He was. He was walking amongst the masses of people who had lived through the centuries. They were gathered all around the outskirts of the smoldering battlefield. The victorious judge of all looked upon those weary souls. He came upon a man who was indeed a tortured soul, his face revealing a life of love and hate. Jesus reached out to the man, but he shrank back.

"Please, Lord, I am not worthy that you should touch me with the hand of love. I was a bad man while I lived."

"Yes," Jesus spoke softly, "but didn't you confess the evil in your life and ask to be forgiven of your sin?"

"Yes, Lord, I did that." The man would still not look up at Jesus.

"Look up, receive your forgiveness, and enter into the distant city of God," Jesus replied. Jesus then embraced the former sinner, which set the universe singing once again. It was as if they had never heard such a confession before. Those gathered there broke into wild praises.

When the singing subsided and things were quiet once again, the Son of God continued walking through the vast sea of the redeemed. He came upon a child standing alongside the road. She was eyeing him quietly as she stood there between a peaceable lion and a small white lamb. The child leaned on the lamb as if it were a crutch. Jesus smiled at the girl and leaned toward her. He reached out and stroked the lion's mane and then knelt down in front of the child.

He looked at her warmly. He didn't appear to say anything in words, and yet it was clear that the child understood Him. "Though you walked with great difficulty through your earthly life, you are now free. Come with Me and enter the great city where you'll never again need a crutch."

He took her into His strong arms and began to carry her so that she could survey her position above the heads of the people around her.

Jesus felt her joy and embraced her. He smiled at her and she smiled back. He carried her a ways toward the city and then let her down to walk on her strong legs. The lion and the lamb continued to walk along beside them. The little lamb was having some trouble keeping up with the procession until one of the redeemed lifted the lamb above his shoulders and carried him toward the gates of heaven.

Jesus led the throng of the faithful into the great hall of the victorious peoples of the world. In the great hall

were elegant tables that stretched far into the distance. It was impossible to see from one end of the banquet hall to the other. I looked at the sea of faces, of all those who had come to join the banquet table. So many of their bodies had borne the scars of being burned or tortured for Jesus. But the joy for everyone was Jesus Himself. His body also bore the scars that had redeemed their souls. They saw their wounded King and rejoiced anew.

I noticed one old man enter the banquet hall. He appeared to be weeping. He had endured many heartaches during his life. Jesus also saw the man. He left His exalted banquet throne and walked toward the man.

Jesus lovingly lifted the old man's face. He wiped his tears with gentle fingers. "Let us only have tears of joy, dear man, for I am your Lord and all weeping is done now. Here, there is only triumph forever."

It was clear! This was indeed heaven. Crying had been replaced with praises.

Gladly, I continued to write.

A hush fell on the room as a great multitude of voices, sounding like the roar of rushing waters and pealing out like the thunder, declared in song, "The wedding supper of the Lamb has come and His bride has made herself ready. Blessed are those who are invited to the wedding supper of the Lamb."

Every eye fell upon the Lamb. We all knew He was the groom. There was no wondering where the bride was. We were His bride, His church, His beloved for all time. Yes, we were His church made up of all men and women, all boys and girls from every age. Our love for Him, and His for us, had made this beautiful wedding possible. It was a union that would never end, a marriage for all eternity.

A final and beautiful pageant took place within my mind. I saw that ugly crown of thorns, the crown that had hurt and wounded my Lord so long ago. Yes, it was there again. In my mind's eye, I watched that ugly crown float about his head, and one by one the thorns fell lifeless to the floor. The crown was instantly transformed into solid gold and came to rest on the head of Jesus.

No sooner was it on His head, than the heavens broke forth into singing a song they had waited centuries to perform. Ten thousand times ten thousands of creatures circled the throne and sang in one loud, glorious voice: "Worthy is the Lamb, who was slain, to receive power and wealth and wisdom and strength and honor and glory and praise!" The deafening sound rose higher and higher and filled the room.

As this wonderful vision of God's revelation came to a close, I saw a new heaven and a new earth and the new city where life and love would reign forever. It brought

me great hope. It was a beautiful city of life-giving trees and crystal clear rivers, golden streets and heavenly beings. It was more than I could ever imagine, more than I could ever dream. The best part of all was that it was His city, the city where He would be King forever.

When the vision was completed, I found myself once more in my little cell on the lonely island. But now all was changed. The wonder of heaven fell like new sunlight on my soul. He who had changed my life so long ago had changed it once again. I can never describe what it was like to be in the presence of my best friend, Jesus. But I must declare His great love to all, so that you too may anticipate the joy of living in His grace forever. Amen and hallelujah to Jesus—to our friend, the King!

"Behold, I am coming soon! My reward is with me, and I will give to everyone according to what he has done. I am the Alpha and the Omega, the First and the Last, the Beginning and the End. Blessed are those who wash their robes, that they may have the right to the tree of life and may go through the gates into the city."

Revelation 22:12-14 (NIV).